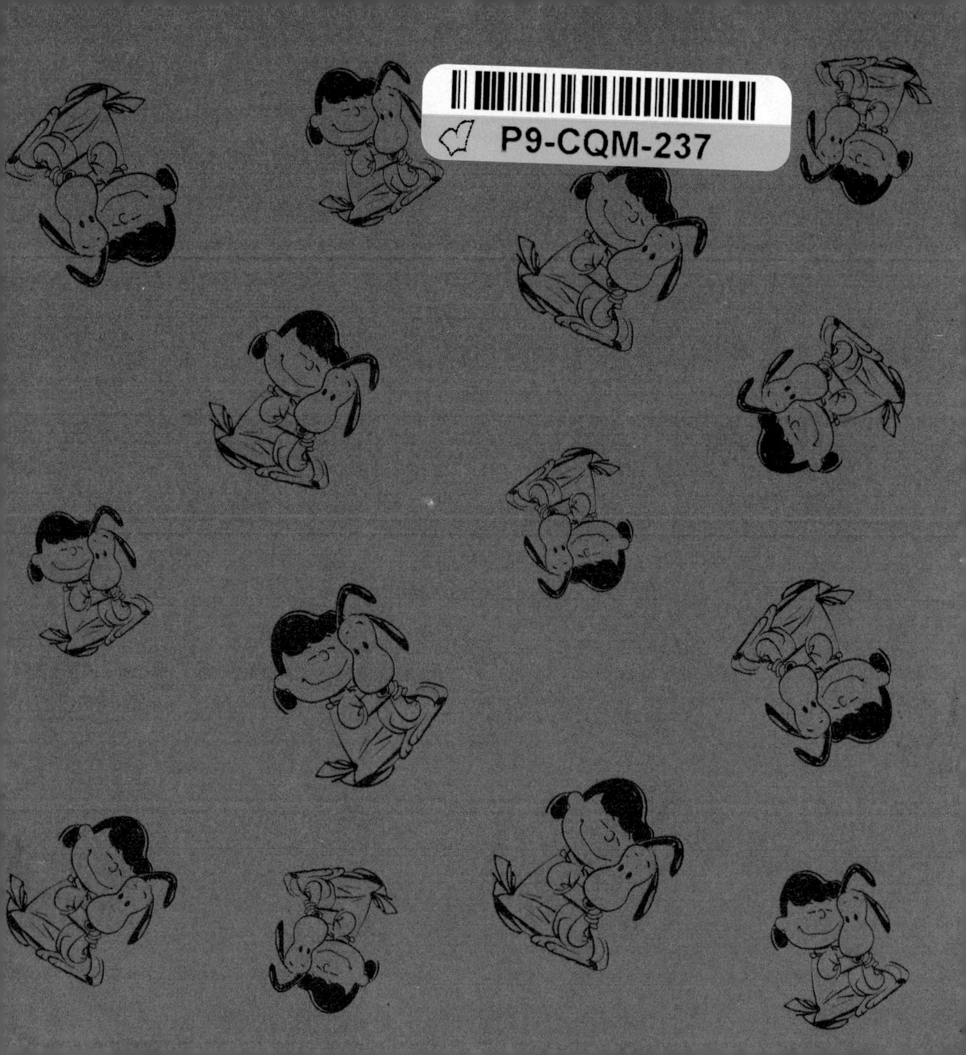

HAPPINESS

IS A

WARM PUPPY

BY
CHARLES M. SCHULZ

ISBN-13: 978-1-933662-07-7
ISBN-10: 1-933662-07-7

This book may be ordered by mail from the publisher.
Please include $4.50 for postage and handling.
But please support your local bookseller first!

Books published by Cider mill Press Book Publishers are available at special
discounts for bulk purchases in the United States by corporations, institutions, and
other organizations. For more information, please contact the publisher.

Cider Mill Press Book Publishers
"Where good books are ready for press"
12 Port Farm Road
Kennebunkport, Maine 04046

Visit us on the web!
www.cidermillpress.com

Design by: Jason Zamajtuk

Printed in Thailand

4 5 6 7 8 9 0

HAPPINESS

IS A

WARM PUPPY

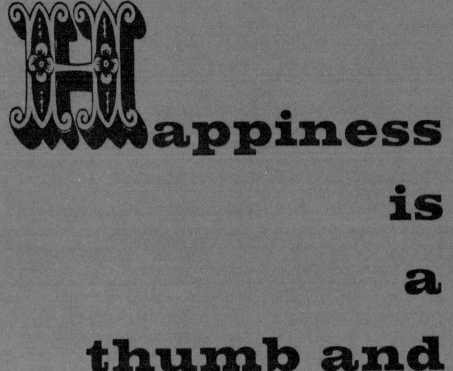

Happiness

is

a

thumb and

a blanket.

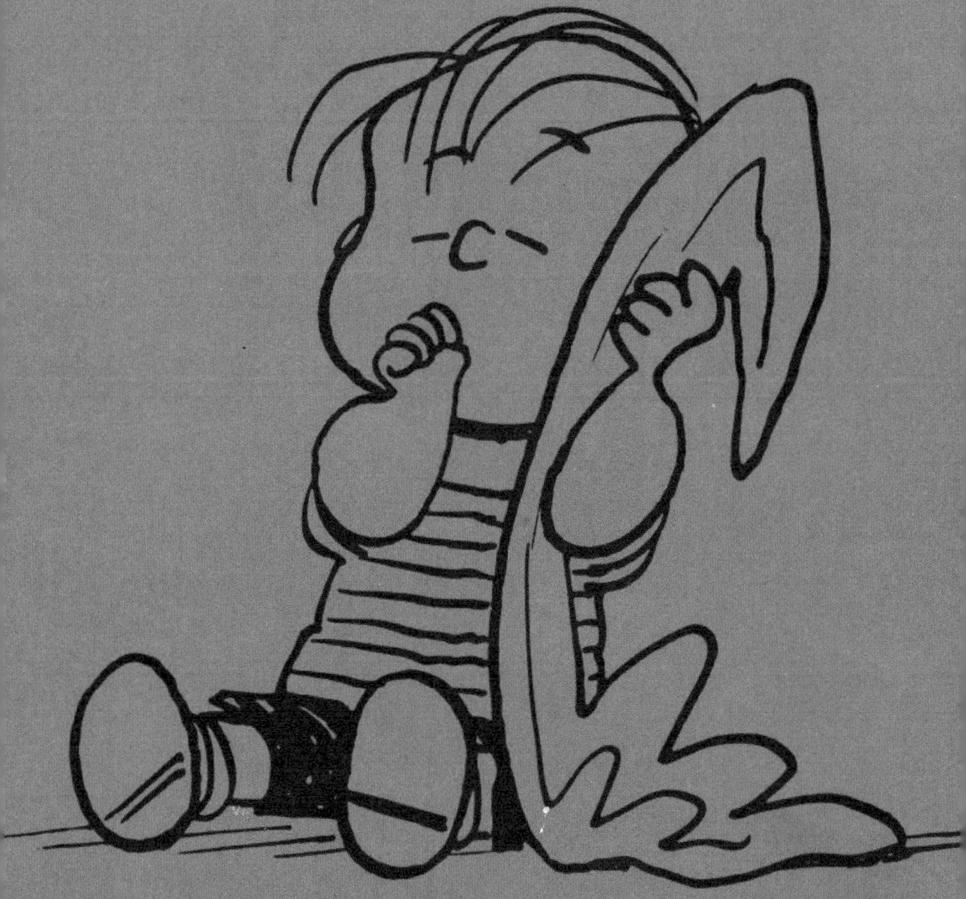

Happiness is an umbrella and a new raincoat.

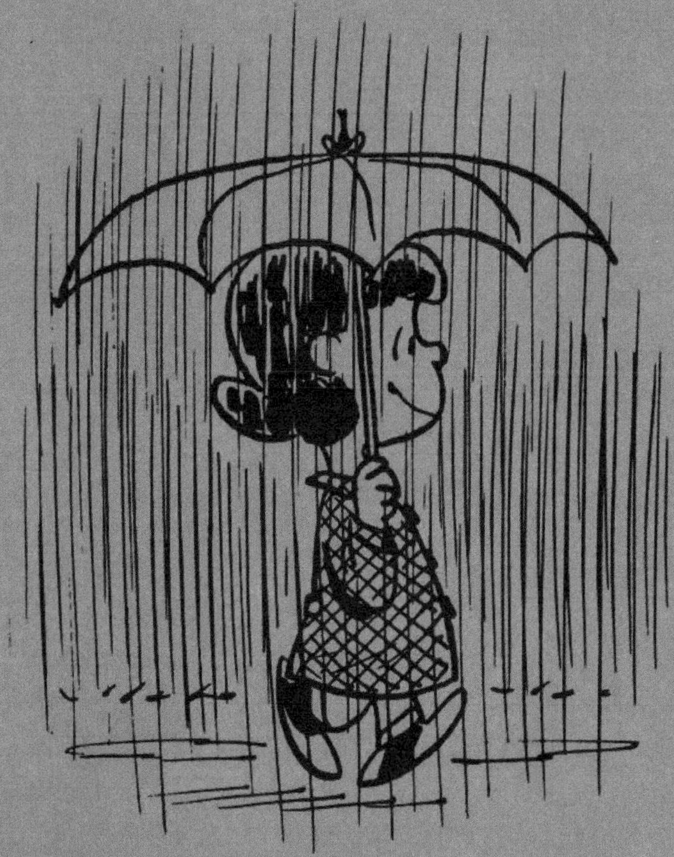

Happiness is a pile of leaves.

Happiness is a warm puppy.

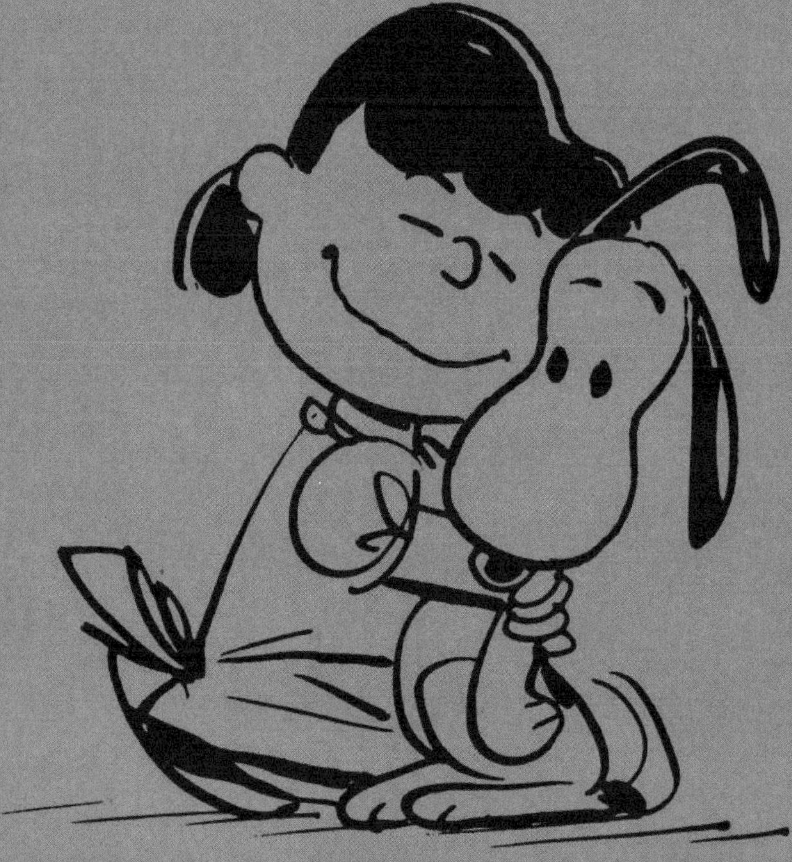

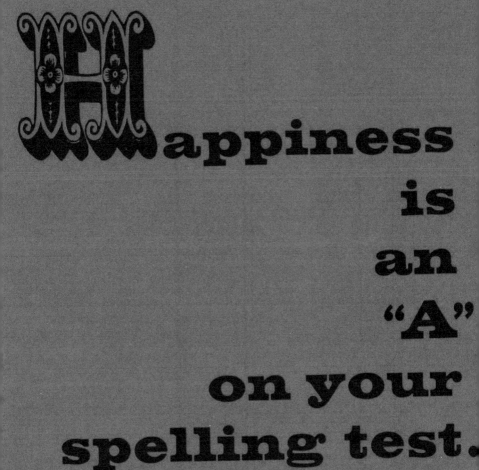

Happiness is an "A" on your spelling test.

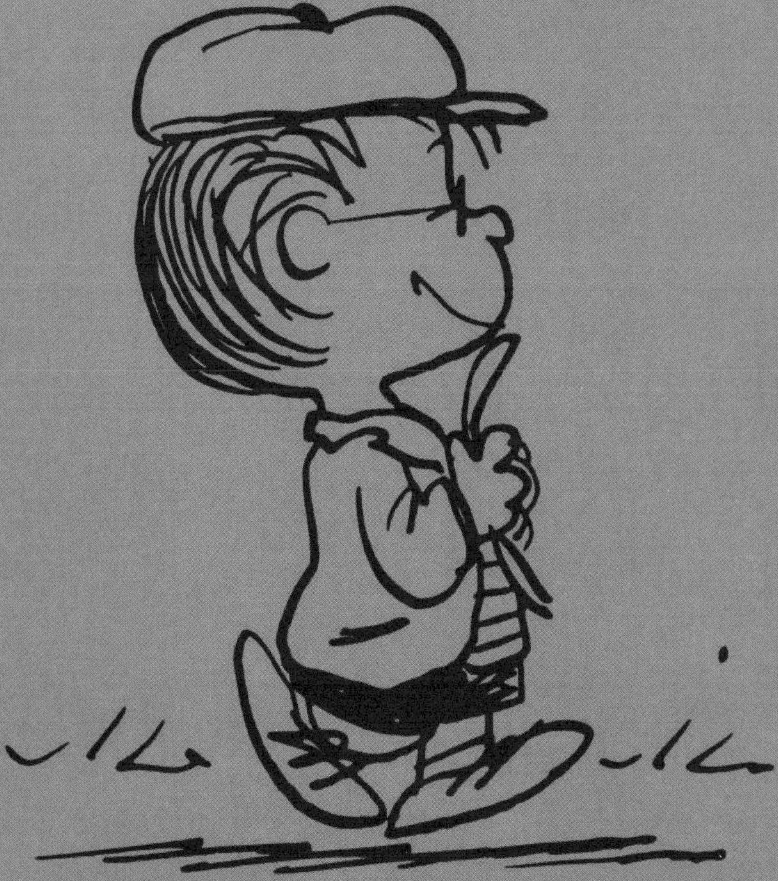

Happiness is finding someone you like at the front door

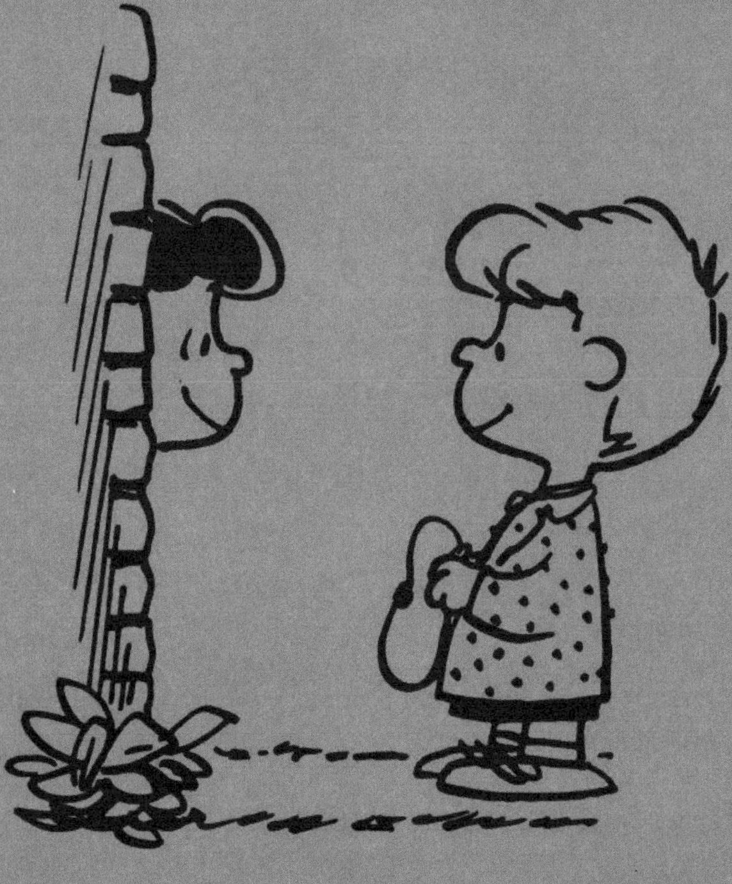

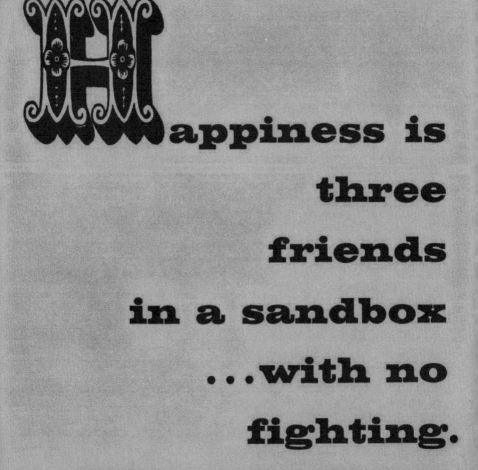

Happiness is three friends in a sandbox ...with no fighting.

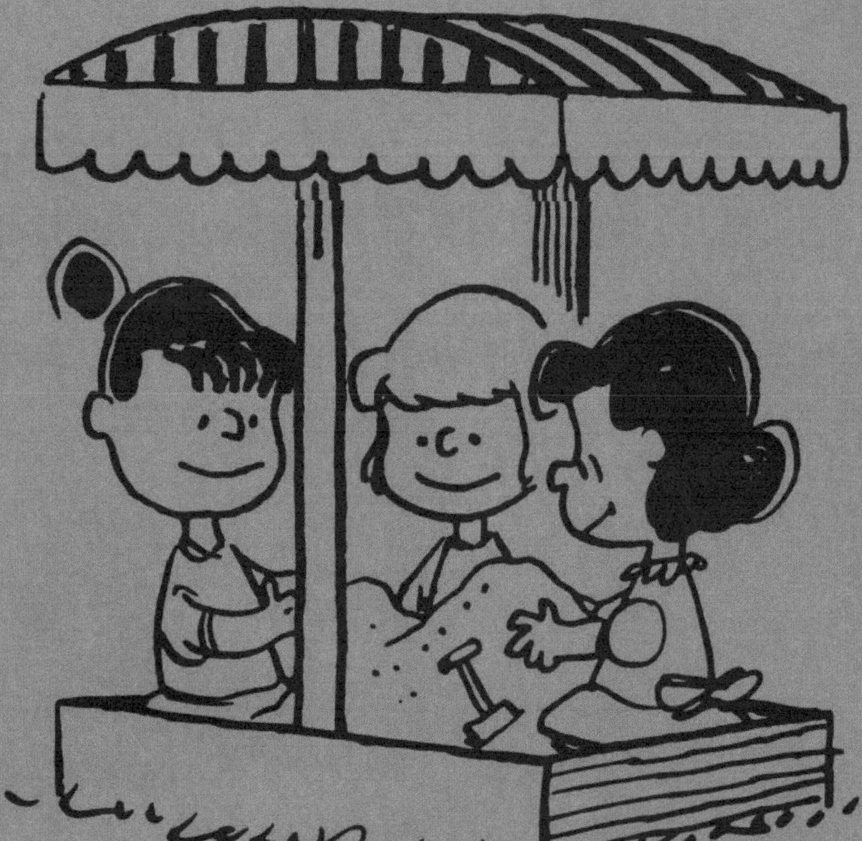

Happiness is sleeping in your own bed.

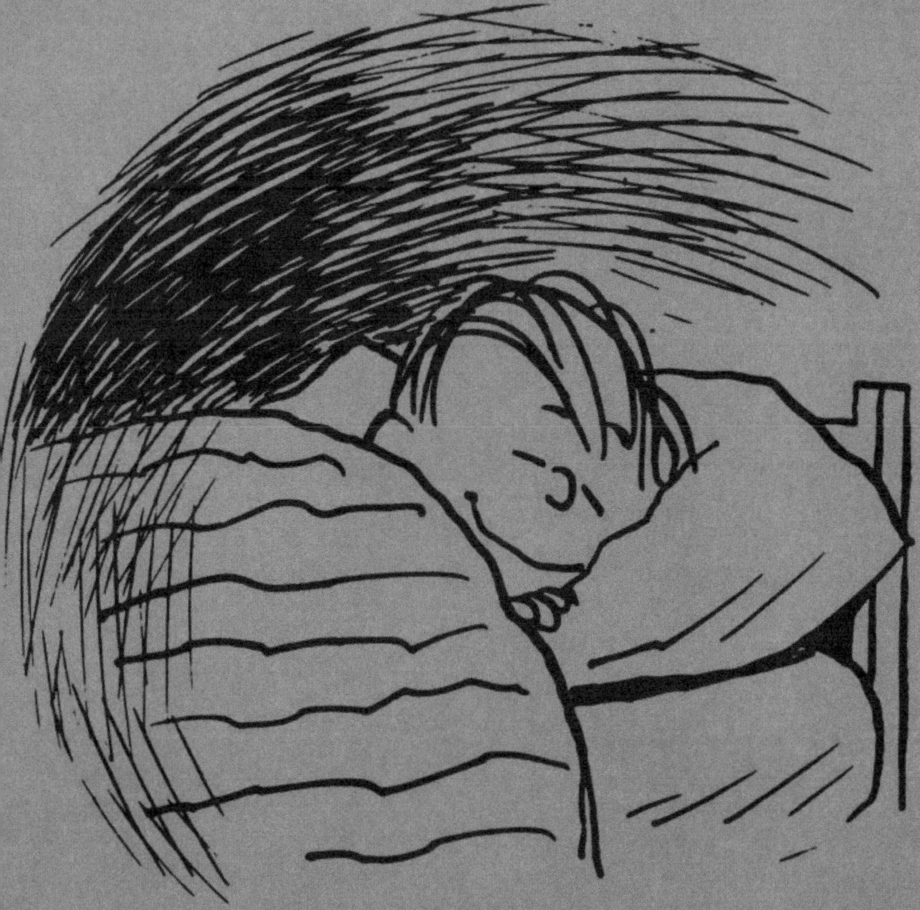

Happiness is a chain of paper clips.

Happiness is getting together with your friends.

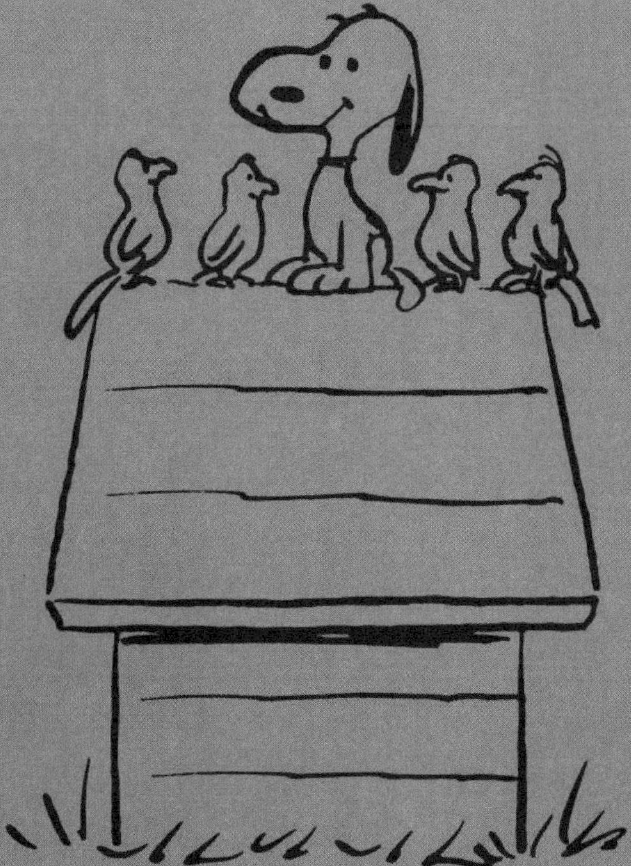

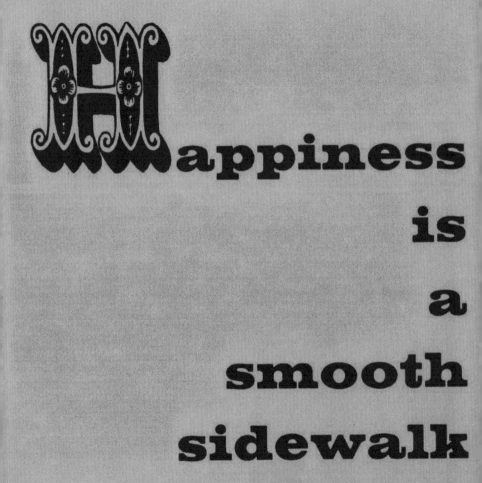

Happiness is a smooth sidewalk

Happiness is finally getting the sliver out.

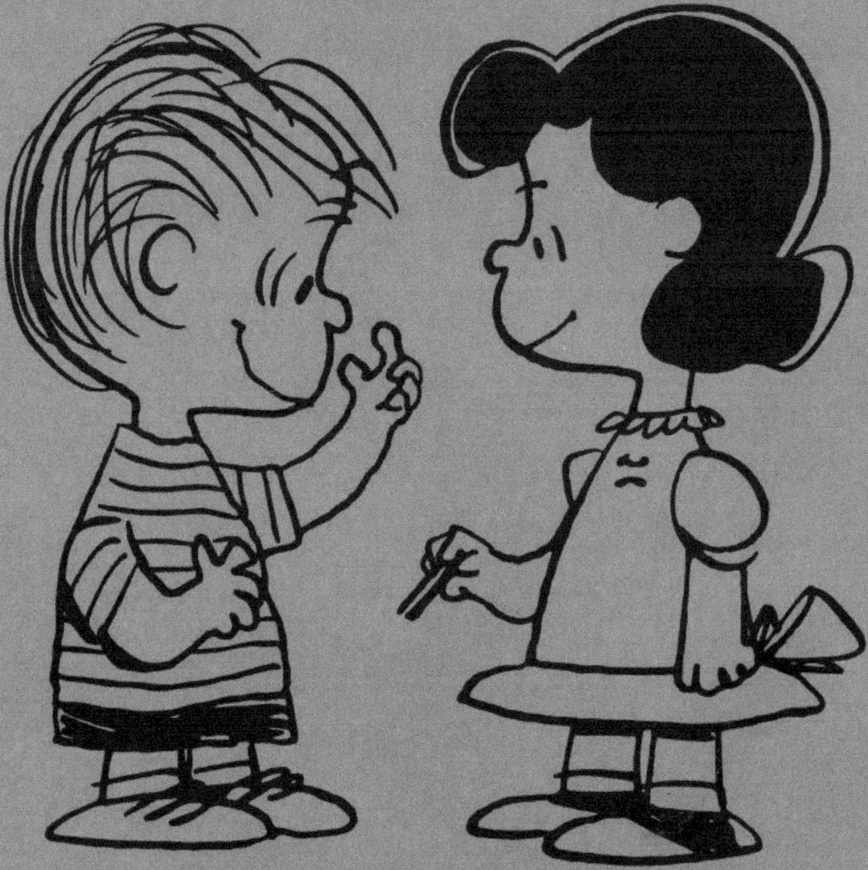

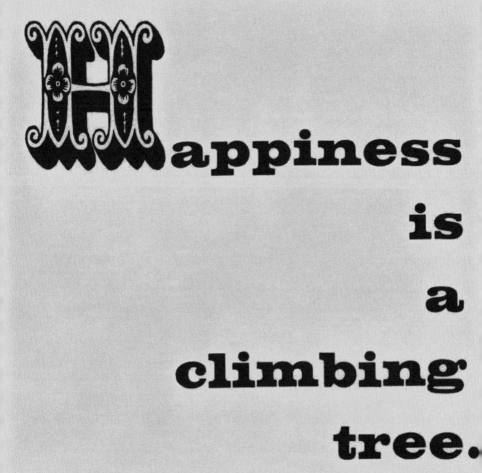

Happiness is a climbing tree.

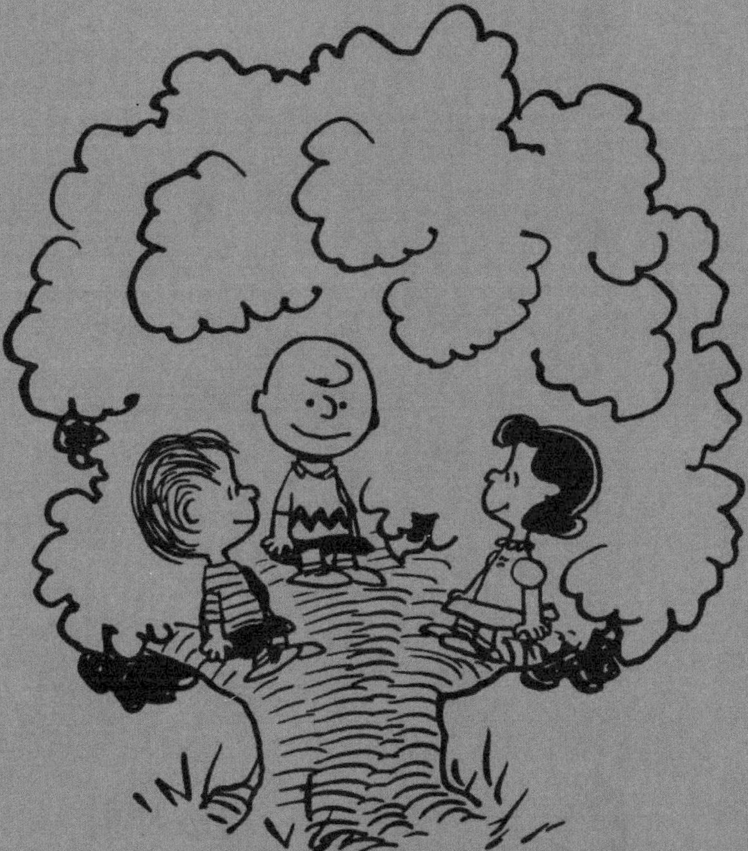

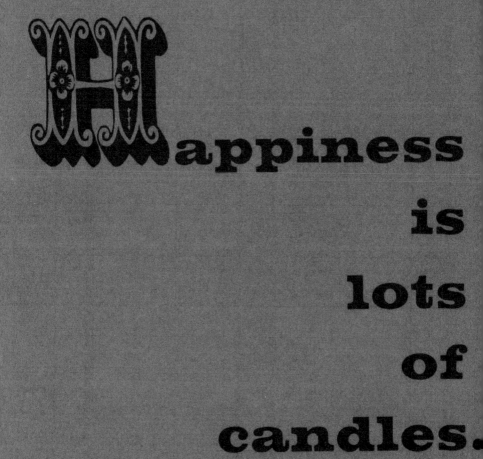

Happiness
is
lots
of
candles.

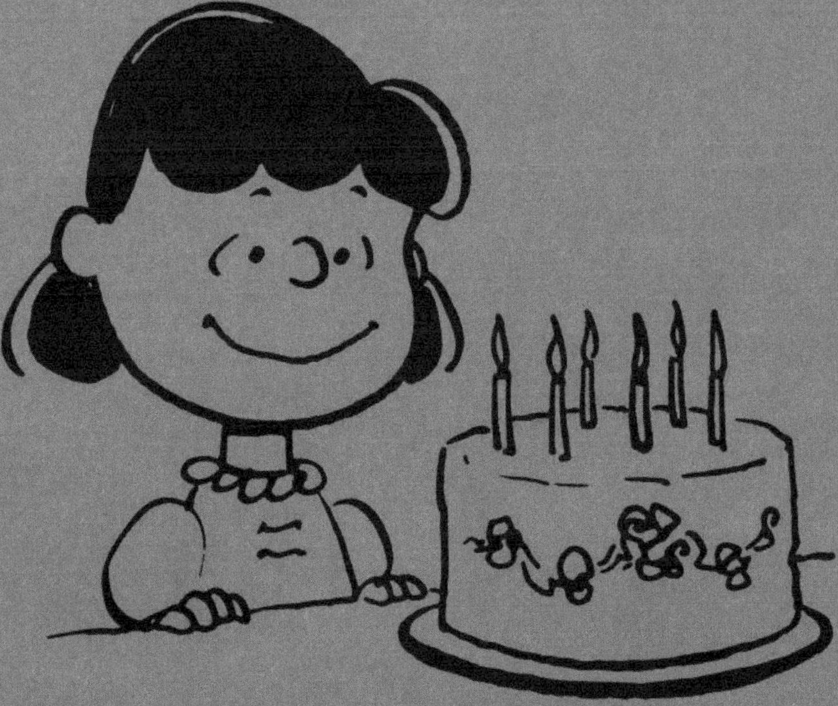

Happiness is being able to reach the doorknob.

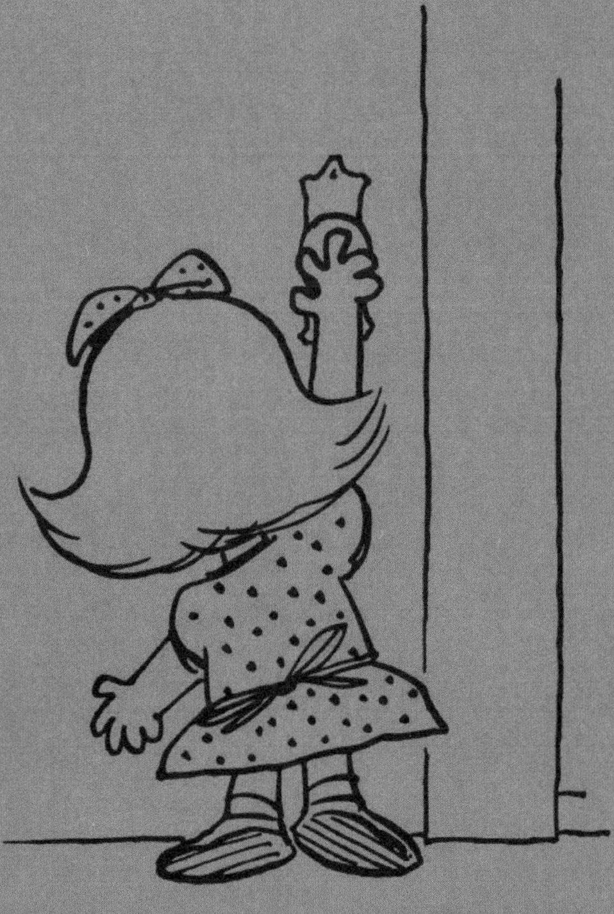

Happiness is knowing all the answers.

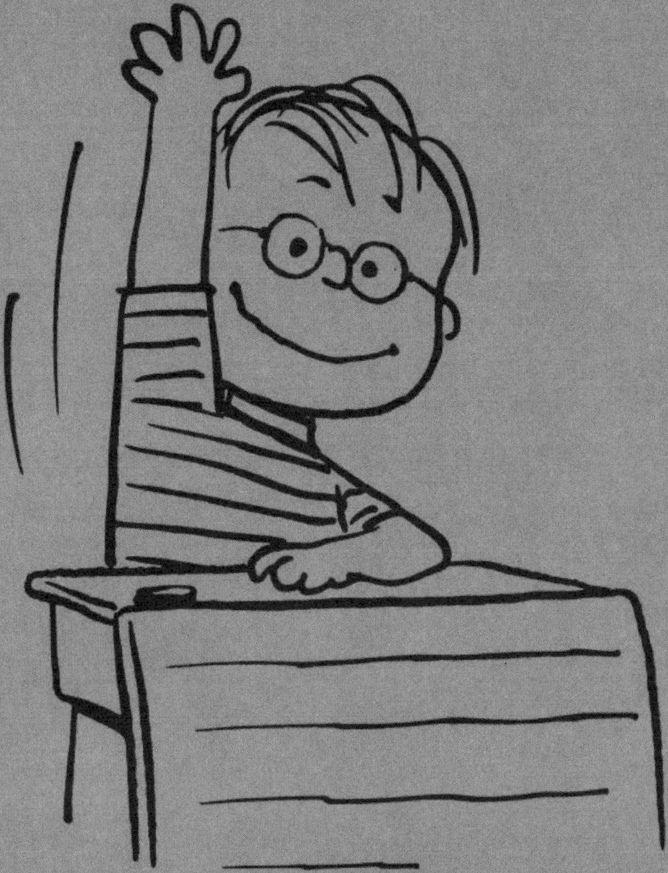

Happiness is a night light.

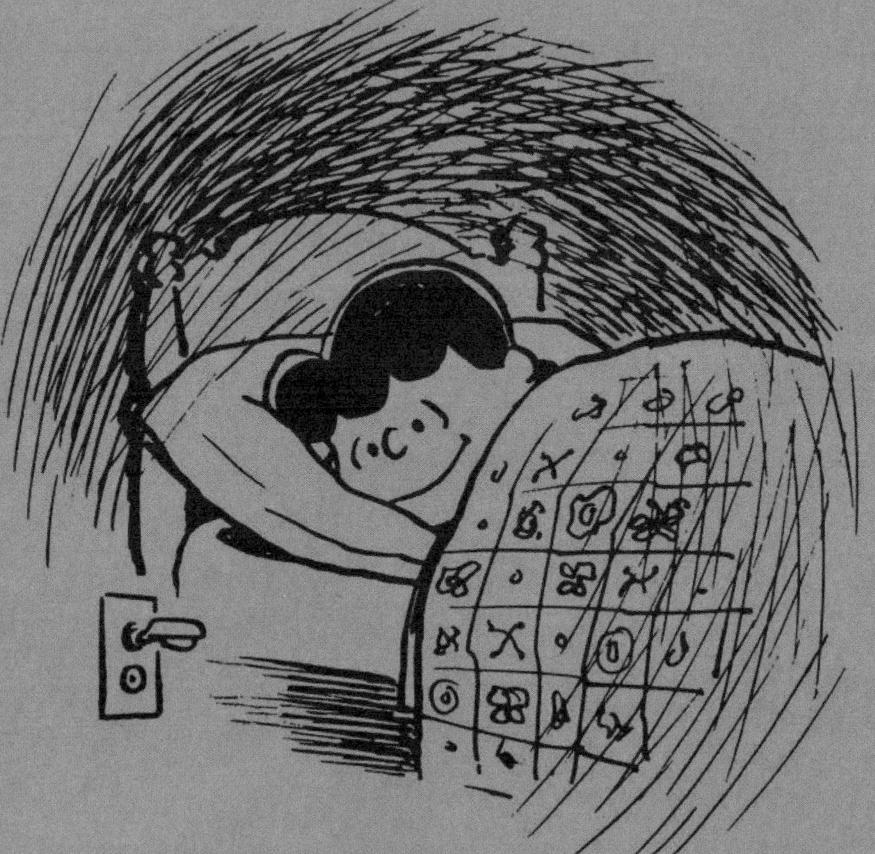

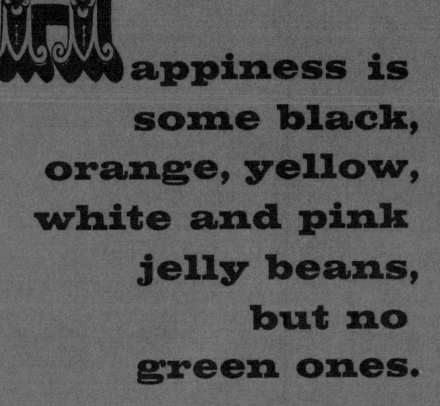

Happiness is some black, orange, yellow, white and pink jelly beans, but no green ones.

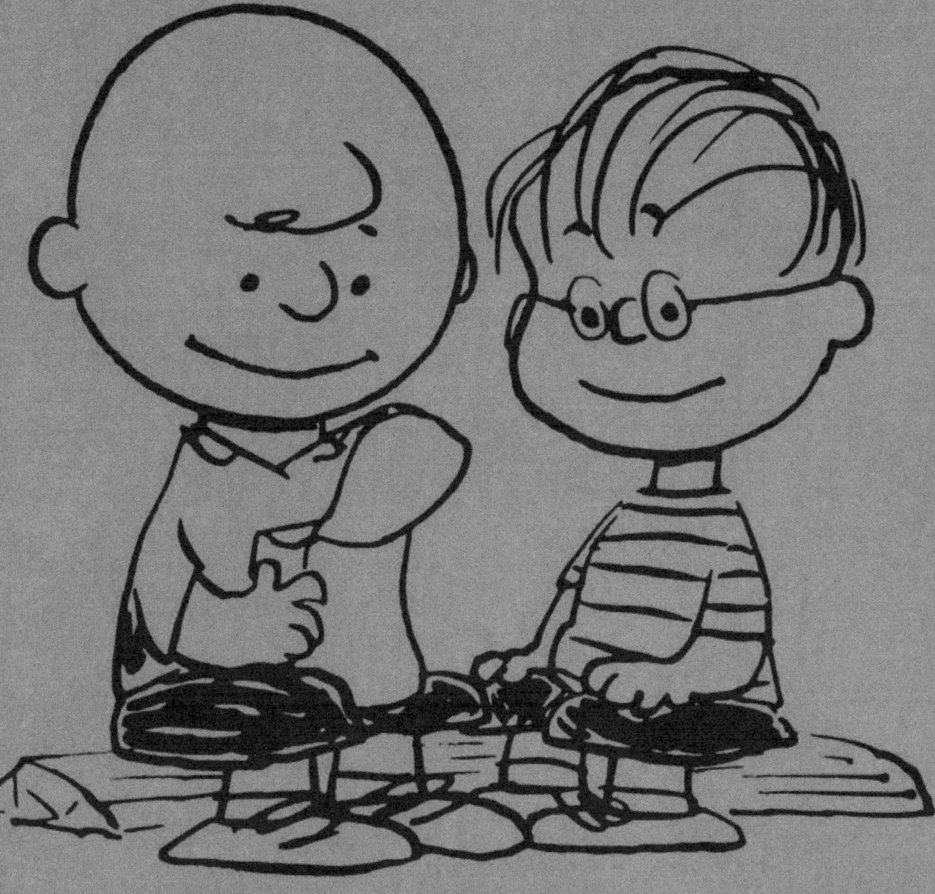

Happiness is the hiccups ...after they've gone away.

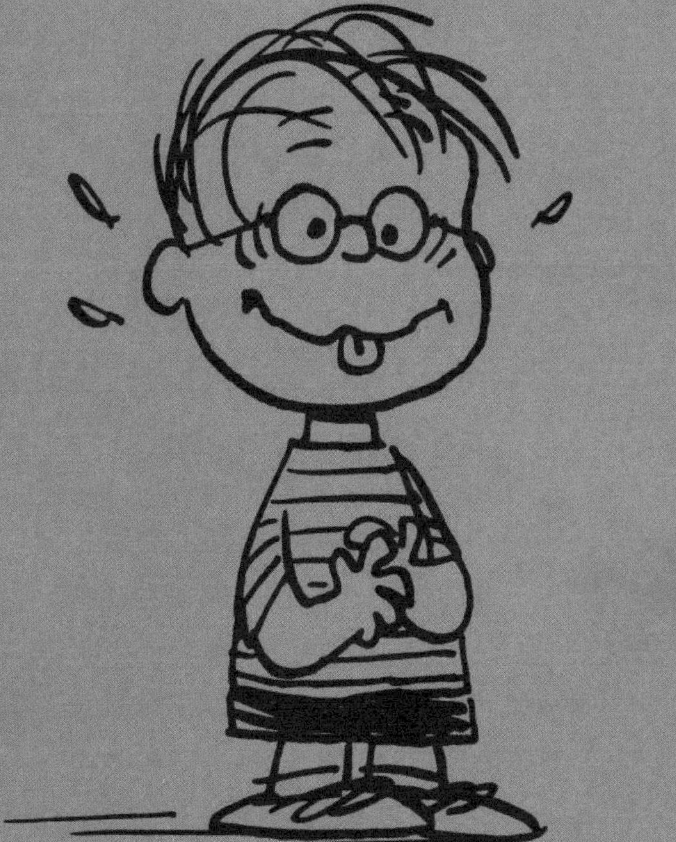

appiness is a good old fashioned game of hide and seek.

Happiness

is

a

fuzzy

sweater.

Happiness is a bread and butter sandwich folded over

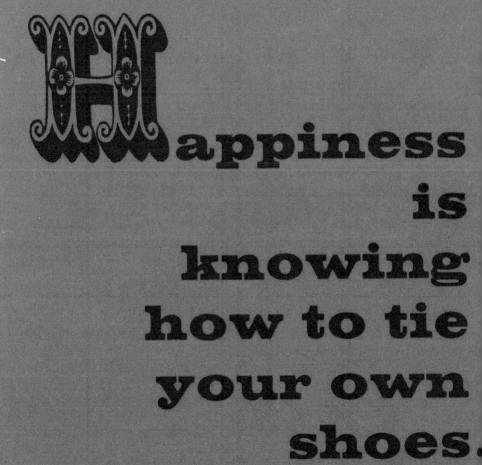

Happiness is knowing how to tie your own shoes.

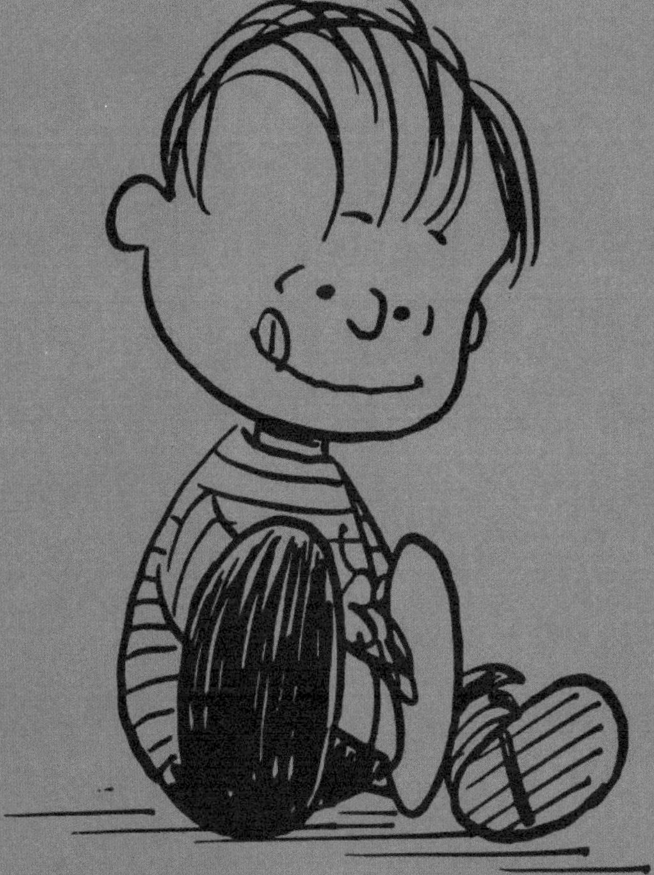

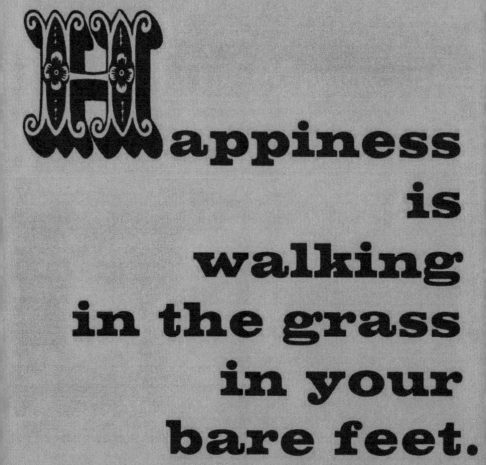
Happiness is walking in the grass in your bare feet.

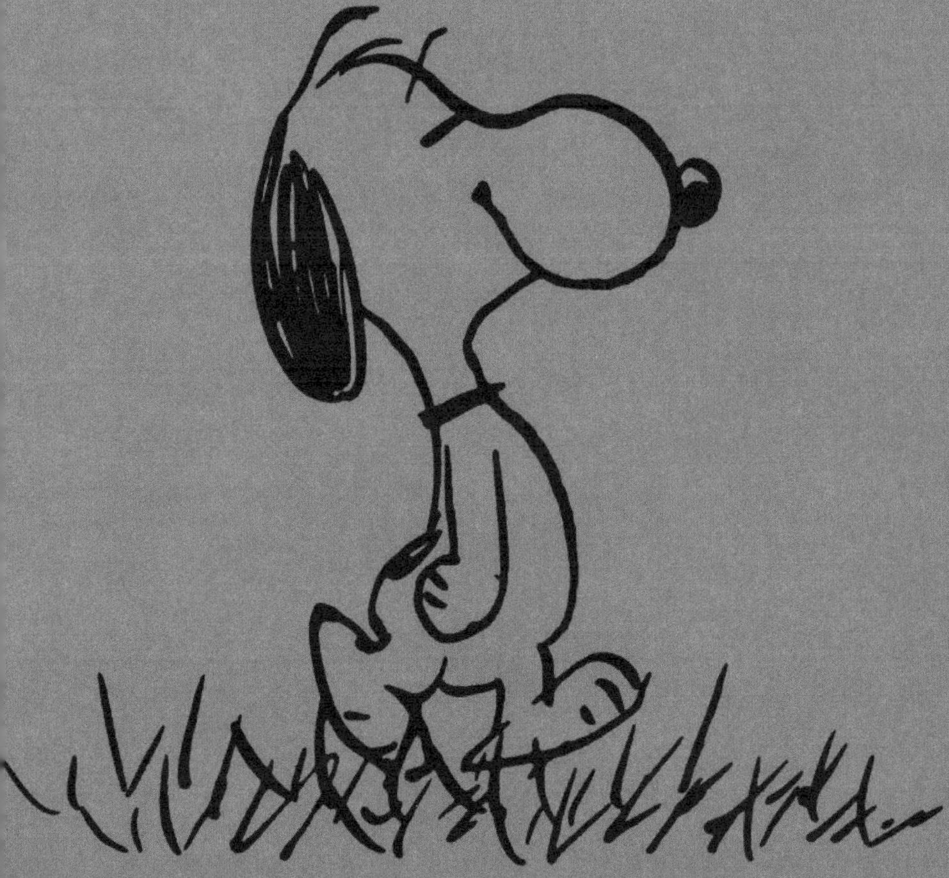

Happiness is eighteen different colors.

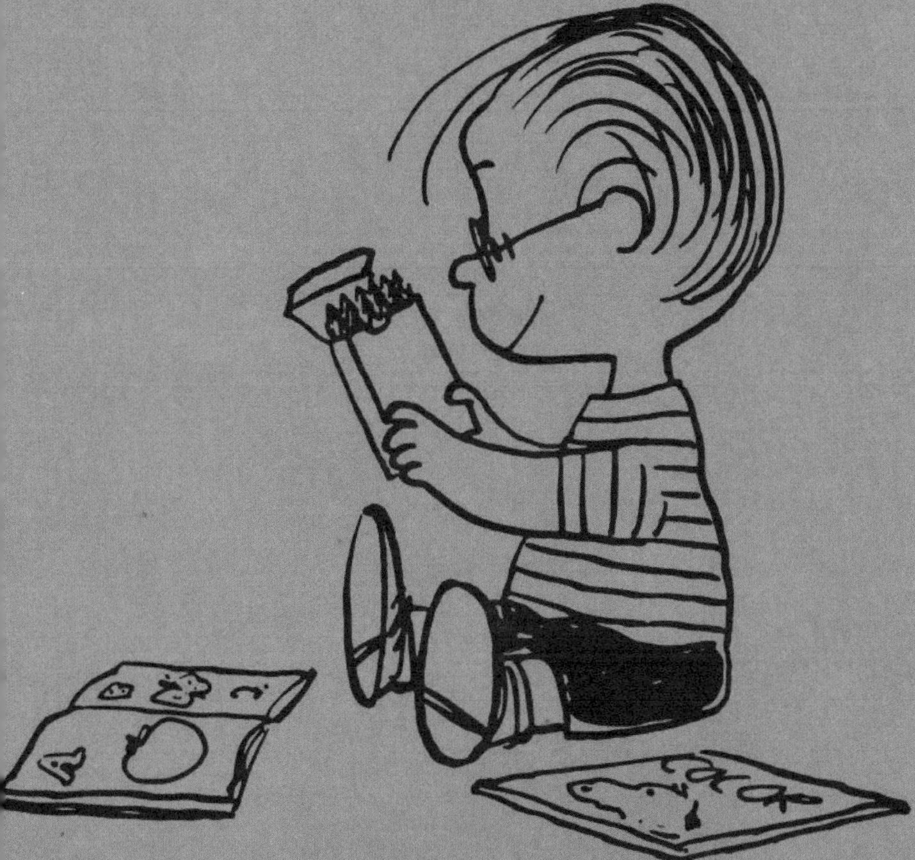

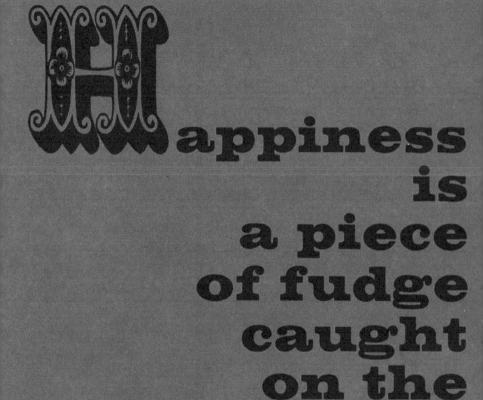

Happiness is a piece of fudge caught on the first bounce.

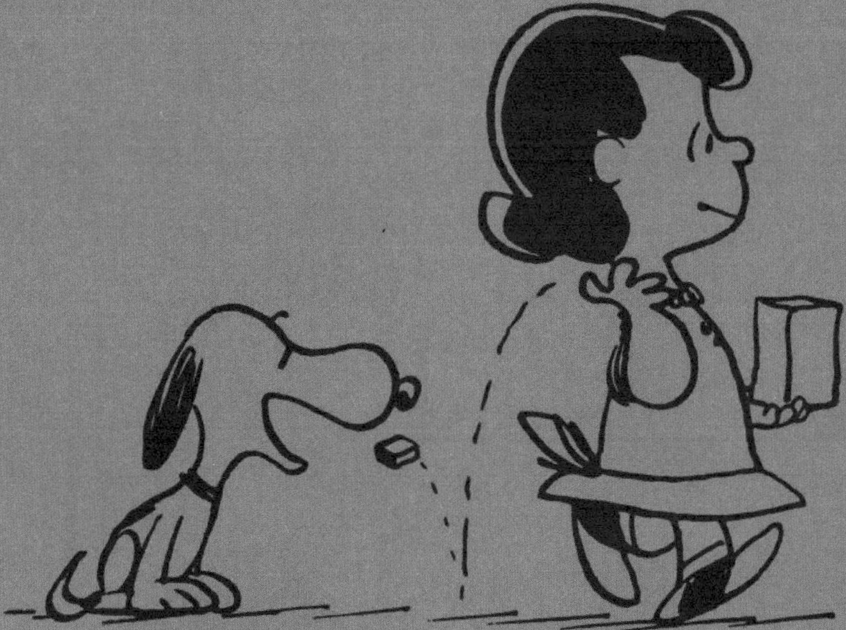

Happiness is finding the little piece with the pink edge and part of the sky and the top of the sailboat.

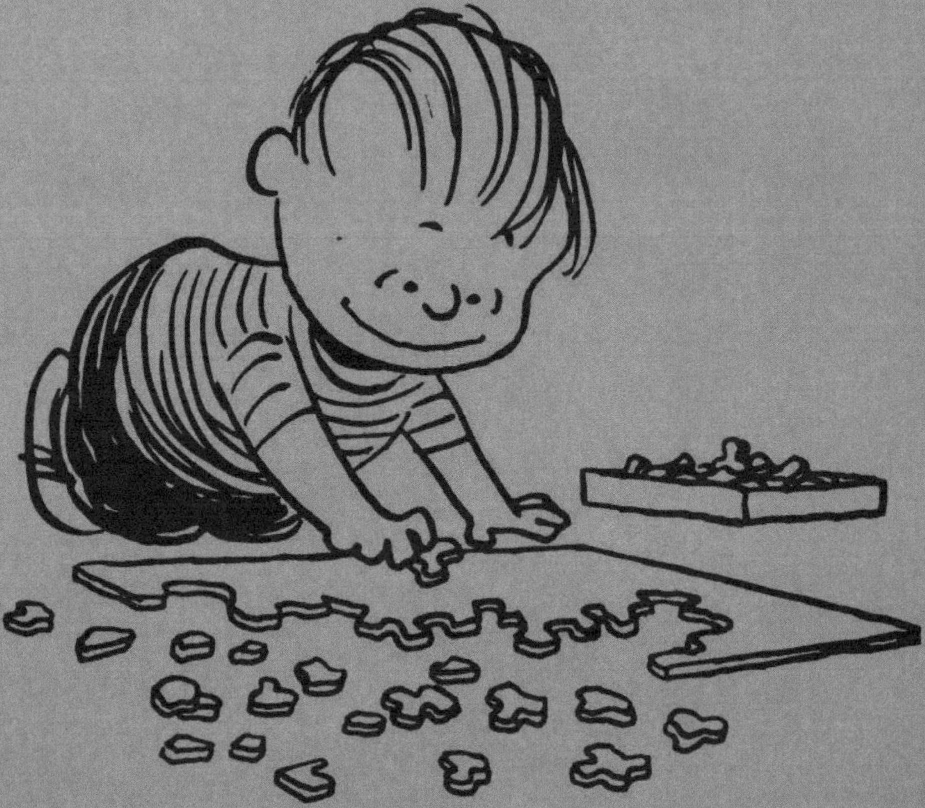

Happiness is finding out you're not so dumb after all.

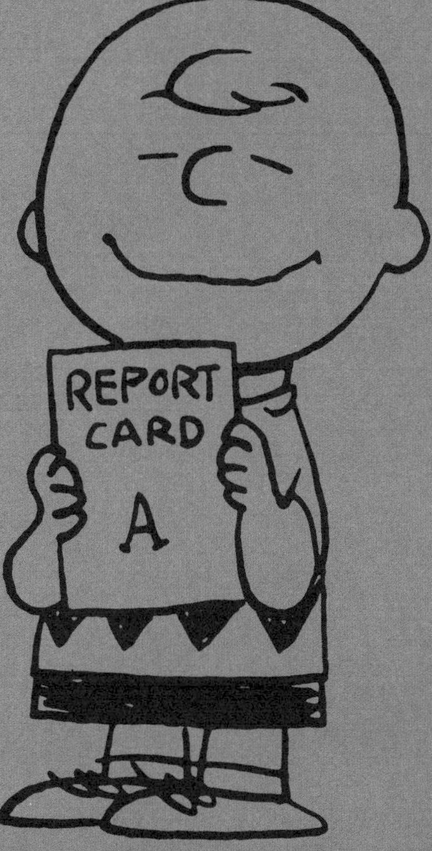
REPORT
CARD
A

Happiness is thirty-five cents for the movie, fifteen cents for popcorn and a nickel for a candy bar.

Happiness is one thing to one person and another thing to another person.

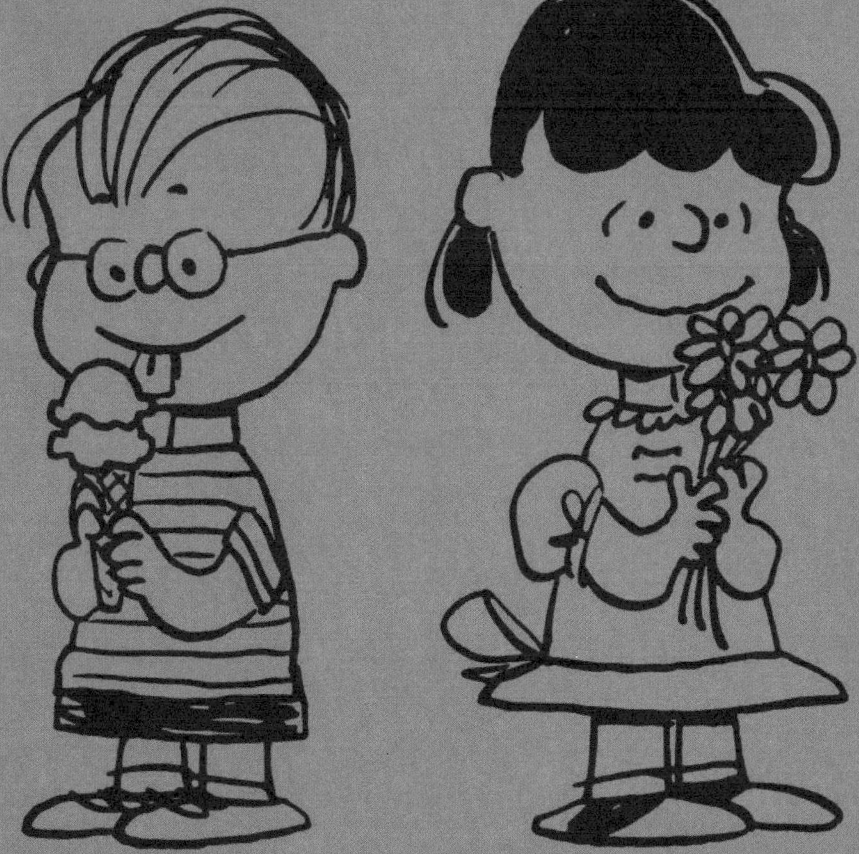

About Cider Mill Press Book Publishers

Good ideas ripen with time. From seed to harvest, Cider Mill Press strives to bring fine reading, information, and entertainment together between the covers of its creatively crafted books. Our Cider Mill bears fruit twice a year, publishing a new crop of titles each Spring and Fall.

Visit us on the web at
www.cidermillpress.com
or write to us at
12 Port Farm Road
Kennebunkport, Maine 04046

CIDER MILL PRESS
BOOK PUBLISHERS

Where Good Books are Ready for Press

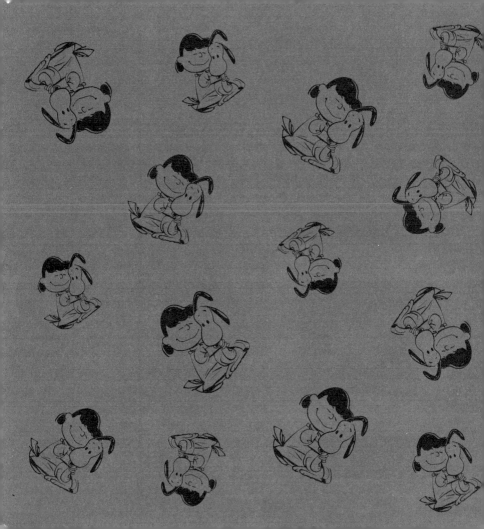